The Strict Economy of Fire

POEMS

The Strict Economy of Fire

AVA LEAVELL HAYMON

 Louisiana State University Press   Baton Rouge   2004

Copyright © 1992, 1999, 2002, 2003, 2004 by Ava Leavell Haymon
All rights reserved
Manufactured in the United States of America
SECOND PRINTING

DESIGNER: Barbara Neely Bourgoyne
TYPEFACE: Adobe Minion
PRINTER AND BINDER: Thomson-Shore, Inc.

Library of Congress Cataloging-in-Publication Data:
Haymon, Ava Leavell.
    The strict economy of fire : poems / Ava Leavell Haymon.
        p. cm.
    ISBN 0-8071-2993-3 (alk. paper) — ISBN 0-8071-2994-1 (pbk. : alk. paper)
    I. Title.
PS3608.A945S77 2004
811'.6—dc22

            2004001886

The author is grateful to the following publications, in which some of these poems originally appeared, some in a slightly different form: *Carolina Quarterly:* "Through the Dark Ranges"; *New Delta Review:* "The Only Way Home Is to Climb Higher"; *Northwest Review:* "Catechism: Om Mani Padme Um," "The Way Down is Steep as the Way Up"; *Poetry:* "God of Luck," "Festival of Lights"; *Snake Nation Review:* "Walking through Luck to Abundance"; *Southern Review:* "Naming Red"; *Zone 3:* "Crossing the Pass," "Rhododendron Forest on the Last Ascent," and "Walking."

The paper in this book meets the guidelines for permanence and durability of the Committee on Production Guidelines for Book Longevity of the Council on Library Resources. ∞

for Molly Crouch Anderson

Contents

Care and Feeding   1

God of Luck   2

Festival of Lights   3

Visitation: Goddess of Prosperity   5

Above the River Ghandaki   7

Walking   8

Moonfall   9

The Questions Women Ask   10

Through the Black Ranges   11

Village of Thieves   12

First Smoke   13

Trick of Distance   18

The Art and Practice of Description   20

The Only Way Home Is to Climb Higher   24

Catechism: *Om Mani Padme Um*   25

Rhododendron Forest on the Last Ascent   26

Crossing the Pass   27

Nightfall   28

Waking   29

The Way Down Is Steep As the Way Up   31

Face of Glory   32

To Climb Mountains, You Look at the Ground   34

Walking Through Luck to Abundance   35

Reentry: Agricultural Horizon   36

Decorating for Holiday   38

Household Sculpture   40

Stars for the Ganesh Himal   43

Bus Ride Back to Kathmandu   44

What Comes: An Offering in Gratitude for a
    Safe Expedition   49

The Question Everybody Asks   50

Naming Red   52

The Strict Economy of Fire

Care and Feeding

Clean your plate, the fire's mother used to say
over and over. *There are starving children
in Asia.* So the fire acquired a taste
for them. When she grew into a bigger fire
and learned she could travel by herself, she found
those hungry brown children mouthwatering.
Truce with her mother's instructions—no worse
than most daughters achieve, so eager to please.

Fire loves all children now, knows to undress them
without pulling tight collars over their heads,
reddens dark bruises from roughhouse fathers,
tickles skinny underarms to rapture, nuzzles
chapped cheeks with that open-oven breath
that carries the good mother smell of food.

God of Luck

Kathmandu: a squat open-air shrine
in the clattering marketplace. I bring rice to Ganesh,
feeling so pale-eyed and conspicuous in Adidas
I hang back and don't present it. Women and children
come and go, chatter-chatter, rub bougainvillea color
on his broad beast's forehead. A dab on their own

to remind them. God of Journeys, Ganesh,
who assigns and removes obstacles.
When Shiva—careless father—sliced off
his firstborn's head, the mother Annapurna
demanded the head of her favorite elephant
and stitched it snug to baby shoulders. A goddess
can't be squeamish. In my pocket, dry rice grains
tick between my fingertips. His tusk is broken,
as always. This is a holy luck

beyond the pair of opposites, failure/success.
It mocks my Western petition for safety. I'm not sure
I can ask for it. Our eyes lock, mine fearful/his bronze.
The marketplace swirls around us—

strange vegetables, thangkas, the smell of nutmeg,
hemp, fat dripping in braziers. Barber clips hair
of customer, both sit cross-legged on a thick banyan root
that crowds the shrine. Air jiggles with bees and gnats.
Right on the ground, a goat carcass is hacked
into pieces—a six-year-old rubs the raw hunks
on all sides with turmeric; childpalms and the meat
take on a deep curry stain. I decide

I cannot make my offering. I decide
to make the journey anyway, to take my chances.

Festival of Lights

Pottery saucers with wicks and butter blink
against the dark, a dark that evaporates
from every threshold. Along the gravel beds
of the braided river, cremation pyres burn on.
High above the city, on gold walls, huge painted eyes
slit open with first light: the Great Stupa
curls its nose at the smoke from below.
                              Eleven men, brothers
perhaps, chant their way toward the river,
bearing a doll bundle wrapped in gauze.
They stack costly firewood into lattice mandala,
lay the tiny body straight, straighten it
again, cover tenderly with straw.
We watch from a distance, foreign women
only just arrived, squint-eyed
against disbelief and the first flare of sun.

It is the Festival of Lights. Since before dawn,
prayer wheels whirl uncounted OMs
into the warming mist. Marigold necklaces
enchant the Cow. This second day is hers
and yesterday the Day of Crow,
the Messenger of Death. Wailing father
leaves the limp bundle to his brothers.
Uncles push lighted sticks at the straw.
Ghee-soaked rags address the sky
with smoke white as prayer flags.

From the old stupa, temple gongs call us to attention.
The Buddha thunderbolt: the radiance of immortality
shines only in the opaque passing moment.
Small girl with one blind eye carries her baby sister

tied piggyback in a shawl. She squats with her brothers
around a trash fire scraped together in the dirt street.
Bare heels inch away from brown sewage water
running behind her.
       Above their heads,
at the end of the canyon street, morning pours off
the cold massif of the highest mountains on earth.
The girl feeds a shred of scavenged newspaper
into the flame. Her face lights up. Her hands uncurl.
In doorways along the street, flames of butter lamps
go transparent in full daylight.

Visitation: Goddess of Prosperity

The fourth night of festival, she comes,
Goddess who grants or withholds,
Lakshmi herself, trailing flame-colored silks.
All the household must be lit

with butter lamps, flames cast
against scrubbed walls. The mama's
hands are red. Tonight will tell.
The night of the fourth day,

she comes. Lakshmi, who decides.
Let it be enough, prays the mama,
her hands red, the butter for the lamps
costly. There is never enough food,

the tiny fires twinkle. Never enough food,
chant the babies. The night of the fourth day,
she comes. It is Lakshmi, to reward
or take away. Elijah drawn to Seder cup,

St. Nicholas to the feast and yule fire—
the old ones warm their unforgiving bones
at the bright celebrations and make sure
that the grave-brittle rules hold fast.

On the night of the fourth day,
she comes. Lakshmi, who decides.
Watch the wick lamp on the threshold
for a flicker at her step. Listen

for the bracelets, the thin coin
of her judgment. Let it be enough,
the mother prays. The grandmother
whispers, from her dim corner:
All fires are burning children.

Above the River Ghandaki

Golden with rice, the terraces
curve around the mountain shoulder,
teeth marks from Kali's comb.
Calm eyes of women gaze at us
out of cream-tea brows, daubed vermilion
to remind us they wake the sleeping gods.

For ten days, they plaited waist-long hair
with scarlet tassels, scarlet for Festival.
Today they scythe yellow grain
with stubby handheld blades, braids
plain India-brown on their backs behind them.
Now as then, their perfect center parts
redden with ocher, a seal of marriage.

In the distance above us all, the Himal reaches
for sky—first a stripe of tundra
parched dun a month past monsoon,
next black basalt, basement rock crumpling up
sullen in the slow crush of continents,
and above even that, the snow. Rim after rim
of it—permanent, remorseless, beyond color.

Walking

> The earth is my twin—
>   goat-footed, she dances
>   under me   then, away

Moonfall

for Diane Wild

For the half hour before dark, we climb
narrow rice terraces, tightrope along paddy levees
instead of bare rocks. Bent low, a woman passes us

going downhill, hands before her weary face in greeting.
She carries home on her back sheaves of grain,
the curved knife she's cut them with, and—could this be?—

an infant daughter. The moon is five days old
and slips over the sky. We are small, closing in
on the upper rim of a deep groove that must be the earth,

the whole earth, shaped like grandmother
thighs opened in a flat V. Far below,
out of the darkening rift, pours the river

we braved this morning on swaying cables, and south,
where all the water will go, mountain after mountain
recedes in mist, distance marked by the thickening

of reflected moonlight. The moon, finally, drops
behind the farther rim. The time for choices is past.
Shooting star! a friend's voice. It has tracked

the lost moon from our side of the wide split to the other.
An arc, she says, *white and slow as a mark of chalk.*
I say, *the wish is yours.* She closes her eyes. In our tent,

the thin canvas floor crackles with stubble
from cut rice on the ground underneath.
In our tent, we tell secrets.

In our tent, I sleep like a newborn
on a shelf in my mother's handmade basket.

The Questions Women Ask
for Joan Welch

Classic mountaineering: we rotate
tentmates night by night, shuffle order
on the single file trail. Accident is inevitable.

In the safety net strung under a high wire,
the give in every knot must be the same.
Women trekkers, we ply a finer web

against ancestral dangers. In the first hours,
we compare cameras, sunscreen, boot lacings.
Later, newspaper questions all around,

where/who/when/why. Later still, confidences
and griefs—families, abortion, partnerships past
and still present, children we've loved, children

we've failed. The matriarch sherpa, Ming Mah,
joins us, and Dormah Sherpa, a guide in training
who still loses her way. Beyond a certain altitude,

conversation stills. We've tossed our haphazard stories
into a no-recipe soup that must sustain us
for the duration. We turn our attention to breath,

dream, exertion. We are siblings, united for survival
under treacherous parents. Our faces watch
the unpredictable ground, the sky. To each other,

we do not speak. The mountains' beauty confounds
our balance, charms us into self-forgetting. Sisters
must be vigilant for each other. The mountains
do not pay attention, and there is no rescue.

Through the Black Ranges

They are just alike. There are too many.
We have walked through them for days.

When we look south, a thousand fall away
toward the Ganges. North, they range between us
and the great ones, the unwatching
snow peaks that keep their distance.

Young mountains, the dark raw color of dirt,
the pointed shapes a child makes, hourglassing
gritty sand through her curled hand, called
inside before she has time to pat it into mounds.

Too steep for villages, bleak even to the woodcutter,
the elms and hemlocks scarce enough anywhere,
and terraces fallen away to scattered chir pine, scrub,
spiky sedge beginning to thin into tundra.

Traced along one side of the sandbox pyramid
by the thinnest finger, a ledge trail twists
in and out, up, down, follows every fold and ruffle.
At last, we stop moving. And now the mountains

lumber past us at the dogged pace of our own walk,
one day's small progress at a time. In the evening,
they grow still, so we lie down and sleep.
Each morning, we are a little higher.

Village of Thieves

A half hour before we arrive, child faces
rim the boulders, squint, turn mean. No signs
or signposts, no writing of any kind, nothing
except stupa, claiming: *sacred place, beyond
good/evil, here/there,* same as every other village.

We trip on rope strung across the trail, a rock
bounces near our feet. This is Tibling, the village
of thieves. Filthy little fingers grab at our backpacks.
Nepali gypsies, we've been warned,
who'll slash our tents and reach inside.

The one-room monastery is empty. An iron padlock
hasps the uneven door, wooden mullions painted
with lopsided mandala, a humpbacked cow,
crooked lotus probably drawn with a stick
against our Western magic, the Wheel of the Law,

not round. Lying in the sun, a bloated dog
gasps now and then, eyes crawling flies and blue glaze.
We turn away toward the painted door again: the lintel
glows red with the face of the Goddess Who Destroys,
long blooded fangs hanging past the door frame.

Something's wrong. In Tibling, it should be
the Lord of Death. We unfold our flimsy maps.
Seventh day walking. Could this be another village?
The peak in the distance might be Lapsang,
not Ganesh. Right before our shamed eyes,

the children's faces plump into giggles and curiosity,
two of them bob on the hemp leash of a panting dog,
rusty locks yawn apart without a groan. We pass
into the Goddess' crimson throat.

First Smoke

i

From hazy blue black shadows, a slanting
first sun picks out creases in the earth
the homey color of pecan shells.
A thousand identical mountains—
I count the one we are on—

and the one next in front of us
sends up a balloon of smoke.
Too far away to show flames,
the plume billows fat and puffy,
then steadies to narrow streamers.

Another puff! woman's voice behind me
in the single file. And another: *Look—a third!*
Who would set such fires? at such altitude,
higher than villages? The smoke slips straight up
against an indigo ground, three birthday candles

lit one at a time. All through the morning,
the lines of white crawl sideways, stretching
to meet for ring-around-the-rosy. By noon,
the ring is complete. The birthday girl has tossed
her hoop. One peak out of all the others burns,
burns upward, slow as an hour hand,
at this great distance.

ii

Cremation fires, Ming Mah tells us
when we all stop for lunch. *This far
from rivers, the dead are carried higher
and burned near mountaintops.*

iii

We must get to water before dark. Half asleep,
heavy with lunch, I force my eyes to the ground
and walk as fast as I can. The fire ring eats higher,

silent as sky signs. It won't move unless I forget
it. Pulling like a noose, drawing smaller
as the mountain narrows. Teasing me:

I look away long as I can stand it—a baby
playing BOO with a scrap of blanket over her face.
When it must be black all the way to the top,

I check again—it hasn't moved at all.
I try to make sense—fire travels uphill, I know.
Beyond that, my thoughts gearjam: deforestation,

erosion, starvation. Scissors/rock/paper.
Hunters, Ming Mah adds, during dinner. *Death fires
are not extinguished, and hunters wait near the peak
with traps, for the animals driven toward them.*

iv

Hunger, hunger, the oldest word
in any language. The sound of it
in English—a lunge and a growl—
passionate infant tearing
good life content
out of the mother body.

Hungry. The hunters are hungry.
Who are we? who are we
to say they must not burn this mountain?
cannot burn this mountain
for whatever little food runs toward them,
toward them away from their fire,
away from their daughter's funeral fire?
away from the fire they lit
with their own daughter's bones?

v

In the strict economy of fire,
all fuel is welcome—first daughter,
last hemlock that holds the topsoil,
nest, seed cone, and moth.

Brush rodents scuttle ahead of it—
field mice, ground squirrel, weasel—
narrow teeth dry, scruff bristled in panic,
their chamois footpads, hooked porcelain claws
not designed for distance running, specialized

through a million loveless years
of evolution to zip ever faster out of sight.
The first sweet smell from the death fire
turning brittle, acrid, as the mountain itself,
peat dry as punk, begins to burn.

Desperation counts for nothing,
their lifelong vigilance burns off
easy as sweat or the esters of flowers.

Their eyes—till now so bright to spot
the hiding places—too nearsighted
to plot the long course.

A hiding place for once not enough.
Even the hiding places are burning.

vi

Kali herself glimmers in the thin red fizz
of burning fur. Final goddess:
her name is destruction and creation
in one word. Mending something,
she is. Just a hem kicked out, another
stitch in time. Pulls the slipknot
in the thread, bites it off, her hag's mouth
filling with smoke from the snuffed flame.

vii

The fire we are too far away to see
eats into the ground, peat tundra
kindled by the sure tinder of childbones.

The fire we are too far away to see
cuts into the woven nests of birds, licks deep
in the tunnels of voles. Encouraged
by last year's leaves, puffing with self importance,
it snatches at the ratchetting heels of the hare.

The fire we are too far away to see
waves its smoke before us, makes the mountain
waver—old trick from early cinema, wobbly frames
that mean time is not linear here, this is dream,
or flashback, or the punch was a knockout.

The fire we are too far away to see
on the mountain we are too far away to climb
in the handful of days we have left.

viii

The day is a long one, and I am tired.
I shoulder my backpack and stump along,
face bowed to bright mica schist under my boots,
grass clumps, patches of snow that slick to ice.

Whenever I stop for breath and lift my eyes,
long smooth fingers of smoke beckon,
one peak out of all the others turns
a cinder wedge against blank white Ganesh.

The day is a long one, and I am tired.
Whenever I stop for breath and lift my eyes—
grainy blue slopes, the steady updraft,
and finally, at the race's end, the hunter.

One peak out of all the others—
I see only smoke, I see no fire.
No mourners, no hunters.
On this mountain under my feet,
no smoke, no animals at all.

Trick of Distance

Hour by hour, funeral smoke edges higher, a circle
ringing the distant mountain. What burns?
The rhythm of my walking takes up
the question. Left/right. *What burns?*

I make pictures in the smoke: mother breast
we remember/can't remember, milk breast/hunger breast,
the mother body we seethed across, small mammals
driven from dry brush, eyes quick for cover, camouflage,

the wish to hide, the wish to stay. *What burns?* I forget
everything. Last night, my book open, flashlight
tied from a roof grommet, tentmate already asleep:
the swinging beam of light snagged the crude drawing

of a snake eating its own tail, and bold marks
THE BLACK WHEEL OF TIME OR DEATH.
My eyes were unlettered as babies'. It meant, means
nothing to me, nothing at all. *What burns?* I have forgotten

everything. *Who am I? What am I doing here?* I walk, I read.
Not enough. A traveler—too much sensation, too far from home—
desperate for facts, codes, names—*What burns?*—too exhausted
to read further. *Answer the questions.* Woman who tried to see

everything, whose memory could not bear it.
Answer again. Amnesiac, her past missing, trying
to relearn, de-scribe, re-mind a world. *Again.*
Shipwrecked girl, grabbing in the dark at flaming timber,

reading at night after her sisters sleep. I forget
everything that is not burning. I must begin again
today, with the cremation fires lively with childflesh,
a belt slipping ever tighter as it nears the peak.

Mouse and rock lizard consumed; hunters,
hungry themselves, wait at the top with their nets,
their pitiful traps. Last night, the fuzzy cracked eye
from the dying battery rocked back and forth

across the two sleeping bags, the soft sagging walls,
the book page. Snake bites its own tail.
Not Buddhist koans or nomenclature of plants,
not Hindu pantheons, not minerals. Nothing

except caption and wheel,
blinking, still blinking today,
through smoke on the next mountain.
Traveler surrenders. Distance has its way:

> *without fire, there is no life*
> *without life, there is no death*
> *without death, there is no fire.*

The Art and Practice of Description

i

The smoke seeps along the ground,
insisting on its own way, like memory oozing
out of the body. There is no stopping it.
Smoke will not be blocked by slammed doors,
by airtight promises, hands pressed over a mouth,
pillow crammed into a howl. Smoke will out.

The smoke insinuates itself ahead of the fire,
tucked secret in the flint, held so long
in the matches, in the twisted fiber of dry wood,
in the fine striation of muscles, hiding there
while cautious memory drafts a story
that leaves out the pain, the other mother,
the bad one with the fire.

A clamor of orders: *describe, describe.*
Voices of sanity, science, voices
of good sense, accustomed to obedience.
Say what you see. All you see is smoke.
This is my body, the answer counters. The muscles
say this, the sinew in the backs of my tired legs.

ii

Does the smoke know it steams into air
the cones and resin of the last chir pine
that holds the topsoil? and the cocoon
of the moth, its artifice old as
the dicot rhododendron leaves it fits
snug as fingers? Does the smoke know

that edge of its birth where cocoon silk
sublimes to light and heat? Does the smoke
twitched in the nostrils of the marmot
know the terror it twinkles against neurons?
the civet fear reviving the nerve path
that shortcuts direct to the brain stem?

Does the smoke reach ahead of fire
the way rage creeps ahead of memory?
Does the smoke fly out of
the blackening char that crosses
the parchment quick as hawk shadow?
Does the smoke read the formal script

before the paper ash curls over? a treaty
of unequals, the covenant
between a vassal and a queen:
I'll help you live if you forget.
I'll give you succor, give you food,
if you never speak the words to me.

iii

Hours, hiking hard, attending my footing
on this icy mountain, attending the fires
on the next. What are they doing there,
whom do they burn? I read so much,
but I am not prepared. My curiosity goes slack,
finally, the ground under my feet melts—
the eldest-child pride, the A-student confidence
that needs replacing with the gratitude
of the meek, if the earth is ever to be reinherited.

My father's intruding touch I feel again
after forty years of perfect dismemory,
punishment in the cause of righteousness
that turned in the way of all torture
to something else, and all memory locked
in the crinoline clutch of the mother, the belle
with the long braids twisted over her poised head.
Hearing no screams, seeing no blood and bruises,
she indicates outside the frenchpane windows—
manners too fine to point—a vermilion flycatcher
come south early this winter, the beadblack eye
of a lizard, hiding inside a curled leaf
to snap up silly gnats.

The image is untrained—*not now! not
when I've come all this way! I'll miss
the odd sacrifice on the next mountain.*
I raise my eyes. Smoke waves its scarf.
Three fires, three sisters.
The first child stretches taller,
a showcase marriage, snapshot children—
better homes, better gardens—
in the hiss of the grubby secret
she cracks like a cheap ceramic figurine,
too ill-built, the incomplete slip joins
and careless pockets of air in the clay
popping in the rising kiln heat,
a failed assignment.

iv

Louder voices, teachers, textbooks,
judges, the unison of those in charge:
*There's smoke on a distant mountain. Nothing
to do with you. Say only what you see.*

I draw up mid-stride. Here's what
I see: They burn this girl, the hunters,
the uncles, they burn her for what
she said, the mother sent them off to do it.

I have withdrawn life from her:
                              the mother's act.
The waste is nothing, the erosion
that will come, the other children who will starve.
*Soak these rags with ghee and stuff her mouth.
Light the fire just there.*

*The smoke from cremation fires
is sacred.* The mother is pious.
The mountain will be made holy again.

The Only Way Home Is to Climb Higher

Night, day, night. Implacable as logic.
The trail steepens, the Black Ranges recede.
In the cold dawn, Ming Mah's voice chants
from her tent, recalls me to the day at hand.
Through the hours of the morning, we ease up
a minor pass on the old trade route to Tibet,
mountain saddle softened a bit by tundra.

The porters stop at the ridge line to rest and smoke.
We catch up with them and lower our packs, smile,
pant, mime, sight along their lifted arms
to the higher passes ahead. We offer trail mix,
almonds, gorp. They laugh and hide
their hands. Stone cairns: other travelers
have paused here to mark the journey.

Whole ranges face away from us on either side.
The sun is mild, tobacco smoke blows
blue and sweet. Beside the stupas
a single crow, the messenger of death,
ruffles her feathers against the steady wind.

Catechism: Om Mani Padme Um

for Ming Mah

The jewel is in the lotus

   The jewel is in the lotus

What is the lotus?

   Where the jewel is found

And what is the jewel?

   what is in the lotus

What is "to be in"?

   that which says how the jewel resides

What is "the jewel is"?

   that the jewel must be believed

What is "the jewel is in"?

   so saying makes the lotus a sheath

and what is "a sheath"?

   Mother walls Mother walls

and is the jewel a child?

   Is the mother not a child?

Rhododendron Forest on the Last Ascent

A rhododendron forest gathers around us,
mother thighs twisting out of the ground
amber and pink, here and there glazed
with a thin gold leaf of morning sun.

Earlier, Ganesh loomed over us, porcelain white,
the long ridge trending off southwest,
glaciers without pity, harsh granite the gable beam
of the world. Now this lush screen enfolds us—

boles the shape of human limbs, muscled legs, a peeling
skin three-colored as the sycamore we know at home.
Ferns, banj lichen pillow the rocks. Giant trunks
of hemlock, burnt out hollow, to crawl in and sleep.

The sprigs of Buddha plant we carry from below
encourage our climb with the smell of tangerines
and lavender. Little seed heads of hope.
We will leave them

at the pass, if we make it there,
at the stupa, if there is one so high,
if we can bear to leave these arms.

Crossing the Pass

A Himalayan eagle turns and turns below us,
tracing updrafts that first lifted days ago
in the muddy floodplain. Our guide Pasang
decides the snow is blown too deep,

our ridge climb to Sing La impossible. We choke off
anger over stymied plans, tedious hours wasted
on map study. Our highest point is only this
minor crossing, and no topo sheets for the new route.

A spirit-drenched country—even minor passes
honored by stupa, piles of granite slabs
without mortar, stacked four-sided
against wind scour, and always adorned:

chrysanthemum necklaces, stalks of Buddha plant,
flapping prayer flags from grateful pilgrims, ashes
of the local dead. Dutiful tourists, we shuffle past,
push our small offerings between the stones

and cross the bald saddle.
There the wind that blows off
China begins its slow erasure of our features.
There the great Himal Langtang is waiting.
A pale moon at first quarter swims up out of the snow.

We turn to descend empty-handed where the drifts
are not too deep, to set up tents for the cold night.
Late afternoon sun rolls clumsy shadows ahead of us.
We turn our footing over to the mountain.

Nightfall

Familiar and lucid,
below the north flank
of the snow mountain Langtang,
Venus rises—

    or what is her name
    on this far side of the world?

Waking

for Karen Whittier

Deep snow blocks the way
we'd planned to go.
We stop and camp
at a lesser pass. A cold night.
At this altitude, dreams visit
us all, dreams of home
and familiar worries:
one woman's stove is on fire,
her daughter runs away
from it, the house is empty.
Another skids down a frozen highway,
all the cars are speeding.
I straddle the huge bear
I've fed and sung to sleep,
massage its violent shoulders
through fusty hide-wool.

At daylight, we wake stiff and grouchy.
The walls of our tents wrinkle
with the ice of our own night breath.
To the northeast, the sun smokes
against the broken face of Langtang
and the mountains leaning up toward Tibet.
Back the way we came,
the Ganesh Himal rears
above us yet, smug,
but now we can see its feet—
the thousand dirt ranges falling away
lower and lower, to slough at last

into mucky typhus alluvium,
the confusion, the crowding,
the billion steaming households
of the floodplain.

The Way Down Is Steep As the Way Up

The river far below us clouds turquoise
with glacier melt, but no silt in this fine bead screen
of infant waterfall, the mountain itself running,
each thin string of droplets easing off
a single tendril of fig vine. The corniche trail
snakes before, then behind the tinsel waterscrim—
light/dark, danger/safety—weaving in and out
of sun glare and vertigo plumb into the gorge, and
shallow grottoes holding the cold smell of mineral iron
and spores of ferns that lean to darkness.

Mist that lofted into slow flight days ago,
rising sleepy off the wet malaria plain
of the Ganges, comes to water only now
on the chill brown flank of this early morning
cleft. It shivers downhill, all elation
lost to condensation, to gravity,
pulled back into the realm of Maya,
delusion, another form of water, another

round in the cycle we'll never escape
while our boots thump steady along the ledge,
our calves tense on the slippery rocks
against that one misstep, the fluid
in our heart chambers surges hard from exertion
and its own weight, lunging systole/diastole,
uphill/downhill, downhill the splash

off this clean rock face into the first of many
dashing mountain rivers. Warming only later,
far away to the south—temperature of blood—
in the sticky mud flats of the huge slow brown river,
the oldest river there is.

Face of Glory

(translation of the name *Kirtimukha*)

The air is milky, solid with light,
an inverted earth that chisels itself
to the shape the mountains leave empty.

Two forms: and our little caravan threads
between them single file, the way a boat travels
the top of the water, the bottom of the sky.

Angry eyes bob up out of recent memory,
eyes carved above the single door of a small temple:
the eyes of Kirtimukha, the guidebook said—

a beast invented by Shiva to crave and eat
some other god whose name and offense
I've forgotten. Voracious stalker, Kirtimukha,

every inch of his beloved to arouse the appetite
for an hour's devouring. But the god I can't remember
prayed for mercy, and Shiva made one of those reversals

the All-powerful are fond of: forbade Kirtimukha
his birthright delight. *What can I do?* the monster
bellowed, starving: *You created me to eat him!*

Eat yourself then, jingled the answer
from Shiva, his attention
already dancing somewhere else.

Scree on the trail rolls out from under my boots.
I sit down hard, more than once. Bound in the caravan,
we bicker, for the first time dislike each other.

I see the brute begin the feast, with his own feet,
his teeth efficient and merciless
as gurkha knives. Move up to the knees—

the seat of anger—pain and rage fueling the hunger
even as it should have been assuaged.
Through the nubbly genitals, the trunk, his jaw

an engine humming the wring of hinges. Spongy lungs,
the brittle hands now, the shoulders—the hunger
become a famine without stomach, without the whine

of bowels—eating the throat, that old howler
of injustice and conflict—finally consuming
the red mouth itself—till all that's left is

eyes. Eyes still dilate with desire,
with need no meal will nourish.
Ravenous eyes I know rolled down at me—

I felt my scalp seethe—
when I stepped through the void
beneath them, to reach the place of worship.

To Climb Mountains, You Look at the Ground

Nobody told me the Himalayas would shine.
Underfoot, an aluminum flourish—the trail
rubbed, burnished, buffed, the scuff
and oil of a thousand years of bare feet
walking into the present at a pace
sustained for millennia, carrying
the same baskets on tumplines—heavy
with mustard seed, babies, firewood.

Graphite, bismuth, antimony, galena,
a mineral shine hazy as old pewter spoons.
Not a mirror where edges snap back crisp,
not chrome to make you flinch against glare,
this is the sheen of child skin, of buffalo-head nickels,
of an April radish pulled from moist earth and lifted
to a bright morning. Of the light source,
not even a shape is reflected—
just the fact of light itself, a glow.

Nobody told me the Himalayas would shine.
My left knee stabs tendinitis with every bend.
The slowest hiker, too far behind to look up,
sweat and sunscreen running under my glasses,
I sweep my eyes just one step ahead, frantic
for footholds, while under my feet, step
after step, the stuff of earth, the stuff of moon,
shine the sun back to me, silver.

Walking Through Luck to Abundance

Frequent stops at this altitude: we share
water, sunscreen, dried apples, chocolate.
Beyond the pass, we no longer gauge
progress by the shape-shift face of Ganesh.

New ranges reach up, pillars of cloud
by day, Langtang here, its shoulders and slopes
still secret, and now and then—
from a great distance—Annapurna.

Conversations are lazy, ruminative.
Are the mountains named for the gods
or the gods for the mountains?
There is no answer, save

we make our way backwards:
Abundance gives birth to Luck,
yet we walk with the child
to find the mother.

Reentry: Agricultural Horizon

We pour like slowing water
into lower elevations, once again
to villages, hand-tilled grain.
The rice is yellow gold, scythe's tang
a soft-metal old moon
lashed to wood by thongs.

Once again, boulders are topped
by the turning faces of children.
Their round eyes flash amber in the sun
as the strange giants toil past.
Namaste, we offer up to them.
Namaste, they call back,
voices like birdsong—
I celebrate the gods in you.

Half these children die, I remind myself,
wondering which of these eyes
will watch the next trek pass.
I subtract one from my own clutch of two
at home, to try out the formula.
Who decides
who goes
and who stays?

Ming Mah tells me that in Khumbu
it is colder, and very dry. The mother's
mother holds each one-month Sherpa baby
under the running glacier melt.
The infants who succumb—
pneumonia, I guess, or sheer recoil
from the shock of life—

die then instead of later,
requiring less wood for cremation
and conserving the tribe's precious food,

that portion of food measured out
on a common scale I acknowledge
only in relict grandmother memory,
a handheld balance beam that must—
even now—be nodding into equilibrium
with the creak of old bronze.

Decorating for Holiday

I almost go by without seeing,
but a card game stops me, played out
in full sun in the opening of a three-sided hut
that fronts the path. In the sepia dark
back inside the single room, a small woman sits
on bare ground, bare feet tucked to one side
in the Hindu manner. She strings flowers
on a length of handmade hemp twist.

It will hang across her house, or swing free
from her house to her neighbor's. Twinkle bulbs
flare weakly out of my dimming memory
of electricity and Christmas. Holidays
are women's work. Squatting between her and me,

the four men pass cigarettes, josh,
deal a hand. Their smoke grays
in noon light, sliced off by the solid shadow
falling straight down from thatch overhang.

My eyes ache from sun. Pasang Sherpa doubles back:
he wants me to keep walking. *They will cheat,*
Pasang tells me, bending into the group to see
how luck is running. He is Buddhist, and another caste—
he has made that clear. He speaks a single phrase
to the men—a joke I don't understand.

Behind the smoke and gaming, the calm brown fingers
have neither slowed nor hurried—a chrysamine
blossom head, pierced through its sturdy sepal knot,
nudged along the twine by finger and thumb. Then
a red bract, tender as the tongue of a child, eased
after it until they touch. Marigold, poinsettia.

The string lengthens. Flower parts line up,
queue of schoolchildren ready for holiday.
The shade is deep, her features indistinct.
Poinsettia, marigold. Sulfur, crimson.
My eyes relax. The colors bloom in her hands.

Household Sculpture

Down, and still down:
the great adventure wanes.
Harvest dust reddens the milder air.
My chest has let go that sense of alarm,
sharp in the lining, and the all-alert light
blinks out. I learn what it is to be tired.

Crisp-edge, jewel-color dreams warm
to conventional fuzzy and opaque,
throbbing symbols relax into easy diversity.
At last, flat stretches in the trail,
ginger lilies, bamboo, butterflies—all these
wait in my yard at home. Safe enough,
finally, for the luxury of homesickness.

The path bends around a drowsy old magnolia—
the tree of Shiva here, the Lord of Death who clears space
for Creation. Like at home, archaic single-stamen blossoms
leak sweetish incense down the crowded leaves.
In the tropical shade, an open hut: someone's house.

And just beyond the shade, a round yoni mound
patted by hand out of wet red clay and
left to bake in the dazzling mountain heat.
Who would make this thing? and why?
Its size and shape, an eight-month pregnant belly.
Mica flake in the hardening clay swings
a tigereye sickle toward the noon sun.

Thick as paste, a stripe of homemade yellow paint
circles the base. For a canopy, limber sticks twist

with a slipknot of hemp and a crown of marigolds.
More blobs of paint here and there, the artist
lulled into happiness. At the four corners,
in play or worship, she's dropped a dollop of petals.

> Seven or eight years old—beyond permission—
> my son climbed the magnolia tree in our back yard
> and cut all the flat platter-sized blossoms.
> On the wood deck, he laid them in a ring,
> in the center the one flower
> unbruised by the long fall. It was
> my birthday. He called me outside
> and there it was: its own bull's eye circle,
> white cream and black-green waxy leaves
> overexposed in the blinding Louisiana sun.

Farther down the trail, I find the artist,
cutting rice, straightening
with a palm at the small of her back
to greet us as we pass. UNESCO
smallpox vaccination stipples
the skin of her shoulder, kiss of an alien.
A toddler peeks from behind her skirt.
I wonder if clay slip dries taut
across the backs of her hands.

My sister. We face each other
across millennia. My people lived
as she does—our words unspelled,
humming free in our throats and in the air,
our losses unrecorded, our pleasures

evanescing in the moment's light.
The kiss she smiles back to me
from all my grandmothers
leaves its own lifesaving scar.

Stars for the Ganesh Himal

      Fires on the next mountainside
      flare the same size and brightness
      as the medium stars.
                       The constellation
      Lakshmi's Bowl sloshes them
      over the earth, a blessing.
                          One flame
      moves, steady as the unflinching firefly
      we followed at dusk, but rising
      slowly as a child walks—
                         up the terraces,
      the curves of new mountain,
      at last into the sky
      with her sisters.

Bus Ride Back to Kathmandu

Betrawadi: for the last time, we sleep
in the clammy tents. I wake to voices:
The bus is here early. The archaic word *bus*
calls up an iron-flanked beast we'd thought
extinct, come clanking out of the Age of Lizards
with rustmetal breath and a mind of its own.

The wheel has been reinvented,
this time with a plastic decal of Krishna
over the dashboard, blue and smiling.
The clear tune from his flute teases us
from our sleeping bags. We strike tents
without speaking, we who have talked
for weeks, all at once self-conscious
at accepting our milk tea.

Across the skinned dirtpack of the road,
up three dented steps, and we are inside.
As I muscle duffle, backpack, jacket
up the aisle, a blood-throb taps in my throat:
I gave my life away to death. Puzzled, I shrug
my bags onto a pile under the back window.
You are always dying, corrects the Buddha-mind.
You are mortal from the moment of birth.

My spine greets like a lost cousin
the civilized angle between seat cushion and back;
my ears, the bygone sound of axle straining
at something that does not want to move,
the grackle of wheelbite on gravel, a lurch,
that boat-launch, womb-carried sense
that the earth's moving under your feet, going
wherever it's going, wherever it's going.

ii

We wave and wave. The bus makes the first curve,
and the porters slide out of sight. Last night,
under Langtang and a moon past full,
we swayed to their songs: *Today I am alive,*
they sing—Ming Mah translates the words—
> *Today I am alive*
> *Tomorrow I die*
> *Tonight I dance*

a modal drone so steady I forget it's not cassette,
the driving *doom doom* of the empty kerosene drum,
and a thump of bare skinny feet hard as the trail.
In the hissing circle of the last kerosene lamp,
a Tamang forced his striped fez onto my head.
His sweat was cold and sour on my forehead.
An invitation, Ming Mah said. I danced.

iii

The bus yaws and rattles downhill,
too fast, too close to the edge.
We have grown used to walking.
We have grown ancestor legs. We have lost
our nerve for this pace, for this century.
The driver is young, there is only one lane.
Entire curves of road have washed away
in the monsoon. Bald tires over scree:
To make the journey. Willing to die.
Krishna bobs ahead of us, taunting, impossible;
American women, and Krishna believes
we are Gopi milkmaids: he will make love to us
each in her favorite way, and all on the same night.

Outside the whizzing window, an elephant-headed
Ganesh presides in whitewash over a village spring,
his forehead rubbed fuchsia. I add to the picture
the broken tusk, the saga of his miracle birth.
Let me go now, I pray to this Patron of Journeys,
first son of the Goddess Annapurna:
I made the journey; I was willing to die.
There is no answer. The pulse of window scenes
does not slacken. The spring where we saw Ganesh
is long behind, running cold and permanent.

iv

Terraces, mustard green and cadmium yellow,
brown fingers of ripe millet, corn kernels spread
out to dry on rooftops. My eyes have forgot
their TV-child sprightliness. Nausea
sweeps through my face to my stomach.
Close up, a black-green magnolia fills
the window. Forbidden to the woodcutter—
cut only by priests for Shiva's drums—
the old tree lowers primitive dicot blossoms
wide and flat as china platters.

The leathery leaves shuffle, and a voice
dooms out of the knotted trunk: *the dance of forms,
that pour out of a void into which they all return—*
drum voice older than Buddha's, signature voice
of the most ancient East—*and always,
through a trick of Maya, pour out again.*

Lacier apricot trees—the window show
does not slow for voices—and blooming plumeria,

whose smell we broke against our hands,
a mash of jasmine and death camas.
The white-flower fragrance comes over us,
dense and opulent. The old bus creaks downhill
into a mist, and it all begins to disappear—

the distance goes first: the hand-built terraces
combing the mountainside across the valley
even out to corduroy, then to nothing at all.
In the foreground, haystacks with crisp topknots
unfocus into brown nondescript mounds.

The mist thickens. We are rolling through
a fading village. Daughters with dotted foreheads
tote babies with wide eyes and runny noses.
Namaste, my face lifts, hands stir out of habit
for the greeting: they say nothing,
they turn their backs and walk away.
I think I see my own back, in a single file
of women—yes! the limping step,
the green backpack!—the woman I follow
along the goat-track trail has waist-long hair
streaked with white, the empty hands
and lilting walk of a girl. Four or five steps
ahead of me, she slips out of my sight

into fog. Krishna's flute falls silent, he flattens
to plastic and cheap glue on the windshield.
Crimson blouses, poinsettias reaching
to the eaves of houses, the reds, the reds
haze over, the fine sharp shades
run together like a muddled dye vat and
leach away, all the same, all the same.

v

The bus is climbing again. I'm lightheaded,
drowsy. Too much altitude, too fast. In the mist,
silhouette black trunks of trees line the road,
limbs hacked off for firewood against poverty
and cold nights. They stump alongside
like cripples, amputees, accusing, accusing.

Now even these are gone. All invisible.
For minutes together, we move
through a bright vapor. All forms
dissolve in a white swirl of dream.

Then, miles and miles ahead of us,
the Great Mother Himal reveals herself
above the mist—reaching languid
in a dry morning sun. Just below our wheels,
the top of the cloud simmers soft
as the steaming surface of a stock pot,
little bit of everything in it, cooking apart.

Above the cloud, we see range after range
rear up solid and confident as crystals,
amber, pink, silver-gold
in pure uncomplicated light. One by one,
the shapes resolve into focus and,
palpable as sound, a few of their names—
the several Ganeshes that loomed
over our journey for luck, Himal Langtang
that waited for us at the pass,
finally, at the limit of our sight,
Annapurna, Goddess of Abundance.

What Comes: *An Offering in Thanks for a Safe Expedition*
(*What Comes* is one translation of The Buddha's name)

Curled in a hole in the flagstone steps
to the venerable Stupa Swayambhunath,
a bony mama dog nurses a single puppy.

Life is always right, Le Corbusier said
when he saw his model tenement crosshatched
with laundry and graffiti. Their bed

too small, mother and pup stuff in
as though shaken down in a sack
or grown overlarge for a womb.
                                          At the base
of the long stairs, the crowded city exhales early morning
mist. Kathmandu again, holiday again. We join
other worshipers to drone up three hundred risers,

women with red tasseled plaits, red blouses, red
striped aprons, vermilion tika-spot on their foreheads,
monks in saffron, magenta, shaved heads, barefoot

children hawking postcards, charms—*Two fish,
Buddha mind, Madam. Mandala from Lhasa*—
the squeak of prayer wheels, juniper incense.

At the top of the stairs, temple monkeys slip
through the grates before the waiting copper Buddhas
and steal the marigold offerings.

The Question Everybody Asks

i

A child's drawing of a mountain—
an upside-down V—
is the picture of no real mountain at all.

Each untidy fling of feldspar, ice, lava
graphs a single history of earth against air
distinct as handscrawled initials.

I learned the outline of Himal Chuli
from the logo of a secondhand bookstore
by the same name, in Thamel. Weeks later,

when the split peak hove itself
across the dirty window of a bus,
it slid right under the two-notch curve

in my memory, the last interlock
puzzle piece, like locating a stranger
by a profile you know from a dream.

ii

Yes, I saw Everest—
twice—on the Thai flight
from Bangkok to Kathmandu
and back. I recognized
the plume of smoke, the savage
broken cheek. *Sagarmatha,*
its name in Nepali: *Brow of Oceans.*

The plane felt too small for me then—
I could beat my arms and shrug it off,
the tight aluminum of the fuselage
splitting along my back like lizard skin.
In Tibet painting, Everest is *Qomolangma,
Goddess Who Wants You to Live,* riding
her snow leopard above shining pink clouds.

Passengers pressed to the recessed portholes.
Open mouths reflected thin black O's
in the scratch-plastic double pane.
Through our own crowding faces,
we saw the first mountain move by,
slow, indelible as a star.

Naming Red

Festival of Lights, Kathmandu,
and the women wore blouses in reds
I'd never seen. *Crimson, magenta,*
the words are wrong. Back home
I find myself reading the sides of Crayolas,
watercolor tubes: *ocher, the cadmiums,
cinnabar. Cochineal, madder carmine*—
I'm crazy for the reds. *Pomegranate,*
says the dictionary, *darker than cranberry,
stronger than average garnet, more blue
than pimento; a tree from Asia.*

And their aprons—loose weave broadcloth
they striped with India barberry, amaranth
planted in their own bean patches.
I pull down Rit dye packages for an hour
in the grocery: *milling scarlet, fulling to wool,
young fustic* (a brown), *vulcan fast red.*
Aprons loomed of ramie, flax, of jute maybe—
which one is it? how can I know?

Ah, my questions raddle a blank desire.
What I want is the fibers themselves,
the fuzz we start with—raffia, cotton—
free as milkweed once, or lint;
what we beat, mordant, groom for the dye;
what accepts the stuff in the funky vat
the way a child absorbs her mother's eye,
fixes it fast inside, changes forever
with the taking of it. A bit of bright yarn
at last, a thread: true, vivid, namable.